YELLOWSTONE

NATURE'S WONDERLAND

BY DOROTHY K. HILBURN & STEVEN L. WALKER

Above: Billowy clouds drift across blue skies over Electric Peak on a spring day in the verdant Swan Valley at Gardners Hole.
PHOTO BY MARY LIZ AUSTIN

5. Introduction

Erupting geysers, hot springs, mud pots and fumaroles combine with dramatic waterfalls, acres of lush meadows, clear mountain lakes, and a spectacular display of plant and wildlife to make the world's first national park the experience of a lifetime.

8. Geography

Yellowstone National Park is located 627 miles northwest of Denver, 529 miles east of Boise, Idaho, 173 miles southwest of Billings, Montana and over 1100 miles north of Santa Fe, New Mexico. It was the early fur trappers, with wild stories about hot spouting springs, who first brought attention to the unusual features of a place they called Yellowstone.

11. Geology

Evidence of the region's formation is on constant display in this very changeable area. Geysers erupt, rivers erode valleys and the wild assortment of geothermal features create a landscape that is indeed unique and other worldly.

21. Wildlife

Bison, elk, pronghorn and deer are just a few of the many species of wildlife living in protected areas of Yellowstone, allowing visitors abundant wildlife encounters.

28. Flora

Yellowstone remains a relatively untouched area and exhibits a fairly unspoiled representation of the region's native plant life including more than 1600 species of grasses, shrubs, wildflowers, trees and other plants.

32. The Festival of Fall

Fall represents the culmination of the life cycle of a leaf. This cycle is revealed in stages as fall touches each elevation of Yellowstone.

35. Winter in Wonderland

Winter comes early to Yellowstone leaving a snow dusted fairyland of frozen waterfalls, steaming geysers and frosted forests.

40. Summer of Fire

The great fires of 1988 altered the complexion of Yellowstone by burning almost 800,000 acres of park forests. Today, the evidence of renewed growth is visible in most every area affected by the fires, allowing us to witness the rebirth of the forests.

45. History

Nomadic hunters may have followed grazing animals into the region during the Ice Age, more than 11,000 years ago. Early Shoshone Indians, called Sheepeaters, were the only Native Americans who lived in the park.

Below: A herd of bison roam across the Lamar River Valley, an area so beautiful it was once described as a place where "contentment seemed to reign in wild romantic splendor."
PHOTO BY GLENN VAN NIMWEGEN

Front cover: Old Faithful erupts at sunrise with Castle Geyser's steam plume in distance. Located in the Upper Geyser Basin, Old Faithful is the world's most famous geyser.
PHOTO BY MARY LIZ AUSTIN

Cover background: Algae grows in the cooler waters of Porcelain Basin pools in Norris Geyser Basin, Yellowstone National Park.
PHOTO BY TERRY DONNELLY

Left: Sunset colored sky and reflections on the frozen overflow of Castle Geyser. Eruptions at Castle Geyser occur approximately every eleven hours and are 20 minutes long.
PHOTO BY TERRY DONNELLY

Designed by Camelback Design Group, Inc., 8655 East Via de Ventura, Suite G200, Scottsdale, Arizona 85258. Phone: 602-948-4233. Distributed by Canyonlands Publications, 4860 North Ken Morey Drive, Bellemont, Arizona 86015. For ordering information please call (520) 779-3888.

Requests for additional information should be made to: Camelback/Canyonlands Venture at the address above, or call our toll free telephone number: 1-800-283-1983.

Library of Congress Catalog Number: 97-66359
International Standard Book Number: 1-879924-28-5

Proudly printed and bound in the USA.

Uniquely decorated with an astonishing variety of natural wonders, Yellowstone was "dedicated and set apart as a public park or pleasuring ground for the benefit and enjoyment of the people" by Act of Congress on March 1, 1872. By these words, Yellowstone not only became the world's first National Park, it became the first in what would become a national park system dedicated to the practice of setting aside special areas, unique to themselves, for the enjoyment of the people.

Yellowstone's 2.2 million acre wilderness is unlike any other landmass in the world, with more geothermal features– hot springs, mud pots, geysers and fumaroles– than all other locations in the world combined. As if these attractions weren't enough to satisfy the millions of visitors who visit the park every year, Yellowstone National Park also contains the largest mountain lake in North America, forests and valleys, beautiful mountains, a petrified forest, enough wildlife to please even the most avid nature lover and the Grand Canyon of the Yellowstone River. There is so much to see in America's first National Park that visitors are advised to spend at least three days in the park in order to experience its many wonders.

Located in the northwest corner of Wyoming, the park spills over the boarders of southern Montana and northeastern Idaho. The Native Americans named the region, "Mi tsi a da zi" which was translated by the French to "Yellow Rock River." Sometime in the late 1700's the area became known as Yellowstone.

It is significant to note that at the time of its dedication as a National Park in early 1872, the American people were more intent on taming the west than preserving it. At that time only one other place in the country had ever been deemed worthy of preservation, Yosemite State Park, established by President Lincoln in 1864. Without the foresight of such notable people as conservationists John Muir and Henry M. Dawes there may have been a very different ending to the Yellowstone story.

Ferdinand V. Hayden, director of the United States Geological Survey, and head of the 1871 Hayden Expedition, was instrumental in the park's preservation. Two others, Jay Cooke, a promoter for the Northern Pacific Railroad, and Representative James G. Blaine, a supporter of the Railroad, can also be credited with playing a part in the preservation of the beauty that is today Yellowstone National Park.

From its fiery volcanic beginning, to the 1988 fires that destroyed 40% of its forests, Yellowstone has stood fast against any adversity dealt by man or nature. With the recent reintroduction of wolves, hunted to extinction more than 70 years ago, the natural balance of Yellowstone remains much as it was hundreds, possibly thousands, of years ago. Yellowstone is the largest relatively untouched natural area left in the continental United States.

Preceding pages: The Lewis River rushes through the rocky narrows of Lewis River Canyon near the south entrance of Yellowstone National Park.
PHOTO BY CARR CLIFTON

Left: Lion Geyser and Heart Spring in Upper Geyser Basin. About two-thirds of the world's 600 geysers are found in Yellowstone.
PHOTO BY GLENN VAN NIMWEGEN

Right: A cow elk soaks in warm thermal waters of Cistern Spring in Norris Geyser Basin. The Greater Yellowstone Area is the largest relatively untouched ecosystem in the continental U.S.
PHOTO BY FRED HIRSCHMANN

Following pages: A rainbow arcs over the mist of the Upper Falls in the Grand Canyon of the Yellowstone River.
PHOTO BY RANDY PRENTICE

Geography... American Heritage Dictionary defines geography as: 1. "The study of the earth and its features and the distribution of life on the earth, including human life and the effects of human activity. 2. The geographic characteristics of an area. 3. A book on geography. 4. An ordered arrangement of constituent elements."

LOCATION...

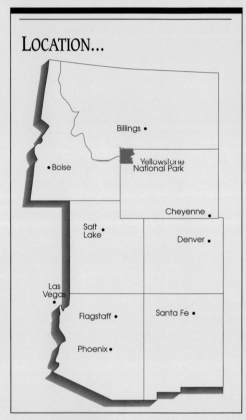

THE CONTINENTAL DIVIDE...

The invisible line which separates the stream basins that flow to opposite sides of the continent is called the Continental Divide, or the Great Divide. The general rule of this divide is that the streams and rivers on the west side of the divide flow to the Pacific Ocean and the streams and rivers on the east side of the divide will flow to the Atlantic Ocean, either directly or via the Gulf of Mexico.

The divide meanders through North America from north to south, from Canada down through western Montana and Wyoming, central Colorado and western New Mexico. It continues on down through Mexico and beyond to South America. It touches both high and low lying areas and it follows the peaks of the Rocky Mountains. There are also continental divides in Europe, Asia, Africa and on the Australian continent.

Yellowstone National Park is one of three national parks in the United States to straddle the Continental Divide.

It should be no surprise that Yellowstone, with its wonderland of steaming geysers, boiling mud pots, petrified forests and dramatic waterfalls should be the home of a most unusual divide occurrence. The small Isa Lake, located not far from Old Faithful, is unique in that the stream that flows *east* from the lake eventually winds up in the Pacific Ocean and the stream that flows *west* eventually empties into the Atlantic. Once again, Yellowstone astounds us with one of its peculiar quirks.

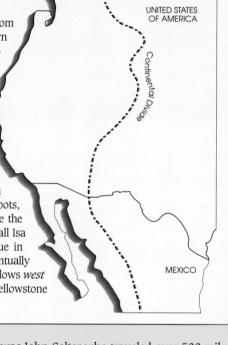

Yellowstone is located 627 miles northwest of Denver, 529 miles east of Boise, Idaho, 173 miles southwest of Billings, Montana and over 1100 miles north of Santa Fe, New Mexico.

The first white man to explore Yellowstone was John Colter who traveled over 500 miles on foot during the winter of 1807-1808 for the Missouri Fur Trading Company.

THE WEATHER FORECAST...

The chart below shows average monthly temperatures and precipitation at Yellowstone National Park. Weather may vary greatly in different areas of the park due to variations in elevations and exposure.

MONTH	AVERAGE MAXIMUM	AVERAGE MINIMUM	NORMAL PRECIPITATION
January	27°	3°	1.6
February	33°	4°	1.6
March	41°	12°	1.6
April	49°	21°	1.9
May	58°	29°	2.3
June	68°	36°	2.1
July	75°	39°	1.9
August	76°	37°	1.1
September	67°	29°	1.1
October	53°	22°	1.4
November	35°	10°	1.9
December	27°	7°	1.7

All temperatures above are in degrees Fahrenheit. Precipitation is stated in inches.

Source: Data summaries compiled by Yellowstone National Park.

Left: Snow dusted pines overlook the cold green waters of the Yellowstone River.
PHOTO: TERRY DONNELLY

Yellowstone National Park has several types of terrain, from the high mountain peaks which reach summer daytime temperatures in the 60°s and 70°s, to lower elevations where 70° to 80°F. is the norm. Evenings are generally cooler and early morning temperatures can drop to the 30°s and 40°s. Winter temperatures

2.2 million acres of wilderness that make up Yellowstone are located in the northwest corner of Wyoming, spilling over the boarders of both southern Montana and northeastern Idaho. National forest lands surround much of the park, including the Shoshone National Forest east of the park. Shoshone was the very first national forest, created by President Benjamin Harrison in 1891. Although there has been a certain amount of destruction of the surrounding forests by clear cut logging, the areas still act as a buffer to Yellowstone's boundaries.

The park has over 1000 miles of trails for hikers of any ability. Short and easy walks or long, difficult hikes can lead to very beautiful, often less visited, areas of Yellowstone.

While most of Yellowstone National Park is closed to wheeled vehicles during the winter, access is available through the use of snowmobiles, snowcoach tours and cross-country skiing for the adventurous winter visitor.

These activities have opened many areas of the park to winter visitors who like to see the wonders of Yellowstone without the cars and crowds of summer, something that is almost inescapable. Automobiles have been the chosen mode of travel ever since August of 1915, when cars were first allowed into the park.

ACTIVE GEYSERS...

UPPER GEYSER BASIN

	HEIGHT	DISCHARGE
Avoca	3-15	2-15 min
Jewel	5-22	5-10 min
Old Faithful	106-184	33-120 min
Plume	15-35	23-70 min
Solitary	5-12	2-6 min
Turban	4-10	15-25 min
Artemisia	20-35	9-16 hrs
Castle	63-100	7-12 hrs
Daisy	75-95	45 min.-4 hrs
Grand	140-200	6-15 hrs
Grotto	8-40	2-12 hrs
Lion	50-60	1-3 hrs
Lone Star	30-50	2.5-3.5 hrs
Riverside	75	5-9 hrs
Sawmill	17-40	2-8 hrs
Shell	2-4	1.5-4 hrs
Spasmodic	3-20	1-5 hrs
Splendid	100-180	1-4 hrs

LOWER GEYSER BASIN

Jet Geyser	3-20	5-60 min
Great Fountain	75-200	5-17 hrs
White Dome	18-30	12 min.-4 hrs
Pink Cone	12-20	8-50 hrs

NORRIS GEYSER BASIN

Echinus	40-90	40-100 min
Little Whirligig	15-25	1-15 min
Steamboat	8-20	1-15 min

All heights listed above are in feet.
Source: Data summaries compiled by National Park Service.

range in the 10°s to 30s° during the day, and nighttime temperatures drop well below zero.

Yellowstone National Park came to be the world's first national park in 1872. The

RARE OR INFREQUENT GEYSERS...

UPPER GEYSER BASIN

	SPAN	HEIGHT
Cliff	2-3 hrs	20-35 ft
Fan	13-15 min	80-125 ft
Giantess	12-43 min	75-200 ft
Morning Glory	Unrecorded	30-40 ft
Mortar	11-15 min	20-40 ft
Rocket	2-17 min	20-70 ft

LOWER GEYSER BASIN

Excelsior	Unrecorded	50-300 ft
Fountain	4-60 min	10-60 ft
Morning	10-60 min	20-150 ft

NORRIS GEYSER BASIN

Constant	3-12 sec	5-40 ft
Ledge	6 Min. - hrs	90-140 ft
Valentine	1-3 hrs	50-80 ft
Vixen	.5-50 min	5-25 ft

DISTANCES TO LOCAL ATTRACTIONS...

Mileages from Albright Visitor Center at Mammoth Hot Springs to destinations within and around Yellowstone National Park by automobile are as follows:

Source: National Park Service, Yellowstone National Park

DESTINATION	MILES	DESTINATION	MILES	DESTINATION	MILES
1. Canyon Village	33	8. Lower Geyser Basin	40	15. Old Faithful	51
2. East Entrance	76	9. Madison Junction	35	16. South Entrance	90
3. Fishing Bridge	51	10. Mt. Washburn	25	17. Tower Junction	18
4. Fountain Paint Pot	40	11. Norris Geyser Basin	21	18. Upper Geyser Basin	51
5. Grant Village	68	12. Norris Junction	21	19. West Entrance	49
6. Lake Junction	49	13. North Entrance	5	20. West Thumb	67
7. Lake Village	51	14. Northeast Entrance	47		

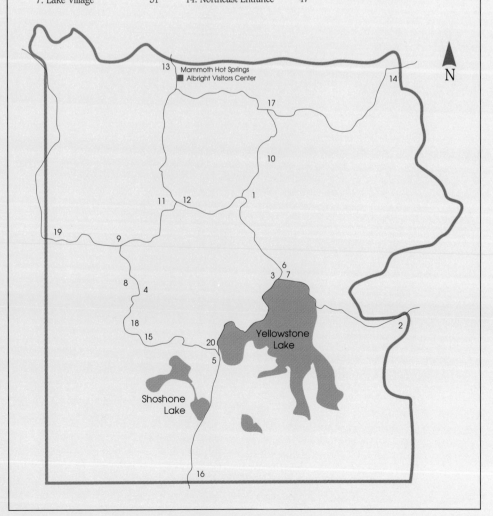

GEOLOGY

The geology of Yellowstone is unique in all the world. Evidence of the region's formation is not only on display, it is remarkable in the sense that its effects and its aftershocks are still occurring on a daily basis. Here, nature is extremely active. Geysers erupt with calculated frequency, rivers continue to erode valleys and an assortment of mud pots, hot springs and fumaroles create a landscape that is indeed other worldly.

At Yellowstone, the geologic story begins a little later than is in evidence in most places. The early igneous and sedimentary formations undoubtedly played roles in the rock cycle–rock material exposed at the earth's surface, brought upward from volcanoes or uplift, was exposed to the forces of erosion which broke them into ever smaller pieces until they were fine enough to be transported to the bottom of the sea. Some particles were reformed as sedimentary layers under seas while others were downwarped to levels deep within the earth and were metamorphed into new rock types under high pressure and temperature, again either uplifted to the surface or rose in a new molten form (see sidebar page 13).

The evidence of earlier rock formations is largely unavailable in Yellowstone as a result of one of the most cataclysmic events in the earth's history. Somewhere around 2.1 million years ago, the first in a series of three of the greatest explosions the world has ever known took place with the Huckleberry Ridge Caldera eruption. The resulting explosion was around 2400 times more powerful than the Mt. Saint Helens eruption of 1980, sending 600 cubic miles of volcanic rock and ash to the surface. This tremendous explosion resulted as molten rock forced its way toward the earth's surface, collected and formed a magma chamber. The pressure then arched the rocks above into a large dome. The magma chamber continued to expand creating concentric fractures. This ring fracture zone extended down to the magma chamber allowing lava, ash and hot gases to escape. After release of these massive amounts of volcanic materials, the weight of the upper crust collapsed into the upper magma chamber from its own weight, no longer supported from below, creating a caldera (large crater). Molten rock again entered the magma chamber and created a new dome on the caldera floor. Ring fractures allowed lava to flow from the magma chamber to the caldera floor. This was only the first of three such events in Yellowstone.

Somewhere around 1.3 million years ago the second Yellowstone caldera explosion occurred in what is known as the Island Park Caldera. The center of the Island Park Caldera is in the western area of the Huckleberry Ridge Caldera, but is outside of Yellowstone National Park to the west in Idaho. Although it is the smallest of the three calderas in the region– it is entirely contained within Huckleberry Ridge Caldera,

Left: One reason Old Faithful is so popular is its consistency. It is known to erupt to heights of around 130 feet and erupts an average of 22 times a day. Every time it erupts, it shoots an average of 5000 to 8000 gallons of water high into the air.
PHOTO BY MARY LIZ AUSTIN

Right: Narrow Gauge Spring in Mammoth Hot Springs reflects the color of the sky above. The spring's high water temperature precludes the growth of algae that would color the water.
PHOTO BY LARRY ULRICH

it is still larger than any volcanic eruption ever recorded during modern time.

The third and last caldera eruption occurred around 650,000 years ago, a relatively short time ago in geologic time. This final explosion formed the Lava Creek Caldera which overlaps a large part of the Huckleberry Ridge Caldera

THE GREAT ICE AGE...

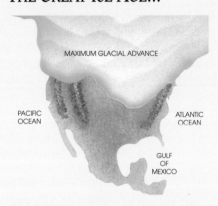

MAXIMUM GLACIAL ADVANCE

PACIFIC OCEAN

ATLANTIC OCEAN

GULF OF MEXICO

Throughout history several ages of glaciation have occurred. The last was during the Pleistocene epoch, forming around two million years ago and ending approximately 10,000 years ago. Great sheets of ice, at times reaching 10,000 feet thick, covered much of the earth's surface. These glaciers advanced steadily south from polar regions driving a variety of plant and animal species south.

A mean variation in average temperature of only a few degrees caused more snowfall in winters and less melting in summers in northern regions. As snows accumulated in snowfields, increasing weight of the snow packs crystallized the base into ice. As ice grew thicker it flowed radially from its own weight. Yellowstone experienced glaciation three times in the last 300,000 years.

THE GREAT CALDERA EXPLOSIONS...

The Yellowstone region is the result of three great caldera explosions, all greater than any witnessed in modern times. The first, and largest, Huckleberry Ridge Caldera, erupted about 2.1 million years ago in a fiery mass of hot gases, ash and volcanic material that was 2400 times more powerful than the Mt. Saint Helens eruption of 1980. 600 cubic miles of rock and ash erupted from ring fractures in the earth caused by pressure built up as molten rock flowed into a magma chamber below Yellowstone. The loss of material in the chamber caused the region above to collapse, falling into the chamber. As soon as this occurred, the process started again with a second caldera explosion, the Island Park Caldera, 1.3 million years ago and the third, the Lava Creek Caldera, about 650,000 years ago.

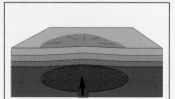

1. Molten rock forced its way toward the earth's surface, collected and formed a magma chamber. Pressure then arched the rocks above into a large dome.

2. Magma chamber continued to expand creating concentric fractures. Fractures worked down to the magma chamber allowing lava and gases to escape.

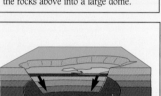

3. After the tremendous release of lava and gases the weight of the upper crust collapsed into the upper magma chamber under its own weight, creating a caldera.

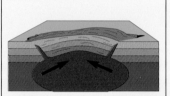

4. Molten rock again entered the magma chamber creating a new dome on the caldera floor. Ring fractures allowed lava to flow to the caldera floor.

and extends 10 miles to its east, is contained entirely within the boundaries of Yellowstone National Park. As the ring fractures once again reached down to the molten magma chamber hot gases and magma mixed to erupt. Ash at temperatures nearing 2000 degrees blew out of the ring fractures covering the landscape for thousands of square miles, instantly killing the plants and wildlife for hundreds of square miles.

240 cubic miles of Lava Creek Tuff exploded from the magma chamber and its roof caved in for the third time in less than 1.5 million years, leaving a caldera 28 miles wide and 45 miles in length. The resulting landscape, covered in ash more than 100 feet thick, was reminiscent of Mount St. Helens after its 1980 eruption.

Immediately following the collapse of Lava Creek Caldera the process began once again. Two domes formed on the caldera floor, one at an area near what is now Le Hardy Rapids and the other to the east of Old Faithful Geyser. As the magma chamber has refilled over the last 650 million years it has produced around 240 cubic miles of rhyolite in three eruption stages

The current stages of the filling of the magma chamber are responsible for the geothermal features we find in Yellowstone today. They are nothing more than new release vents along the ring fractures above the magma chamber.

Yellowstone has more than 10,000 geothermal features, approximately 300 of these features are geysers, a concentration unequalled in all the rest of the world's geyser fields combined. The earth's crust is thinner in the Yellowstone area

Above: Great Fountain Geyser is one of Yellowstone National Park's largest fountain geysers.
PHOTO BY DICK DIETRICH

than most other areas, bringing magma closer to the surface, causing Yellowstone to be one of the hottest places on the earth.

Scientists have drilled into Norris Geyser Basin and found the temperature as hot as 459° F at a depth of only 1087 feet. As rain or snow melt seeps into the ground and begins a slow journey into the earth it is heated by the earth's

temperature above the magma chamber by about one degree Fahrenheit for every 100 feet it in depth. Because of the increased pressure deep below the earth's surface the water reaches temperatures far above the normal boiling point of 212° without turning from a liquid to

INNER WORKINGS OF A GEYSER...

A certain combination of circumstances must combine to create a geyser, including an abundant source of water; an underground plumbing system with constricted areas built up by the mineral geyserite; and a heat source.

Surface water from rain and snowmelt seeps deep down into the ground where it comes into contact with super heated rocks. Rocks this hot can only be found in areas with fairly recent volcanic activity. Instead of turning into steam, as it normally would, the water stays liquid because of the pressure exerted from the weight of the earth above.

The pressurized hot water dissolves minerals within the surrounding rock and silicon dioxide, also called silica, builds up over time to block the underground channels, creating a narrow area often close to the surface. More water from above puts pressure on the heated water below and eventually the boiling water erupts.

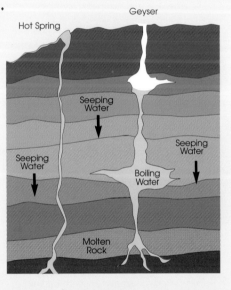

Hot Spring   Geyser

Seeping Water

Seeping Water

Seeping Water

Boiling Water

Molten Rock

THE ROCK CYCLE...

Rock material exposed at the surface of the earth, brought upward by volcanoes or uplift, is constantly exposed to forces of erosion which break the rocks into ever finer pieces that are transported, by water or wind, to the sea. The sediments are then deposited on the sea bed where their weight may cause the region to sag, forming a geosyncline.

When downwarping is continued over a long period of time, resulting pressures will convert the rock into new formations. At depths greater than 25 miles, a deep metamorphism, from high pressure and temperature, causes re-crystallization and converts the original sediments to complex new rock types. These rocks then start their own uplift cycle to the earth's surface.

Melting of metamorphic rock deep in the earth's crust generates new granitic magma, which as molten lava migrates to the surface. Magma extrudes through the earth's surface fissures or erupts from volcanoes forming igneous rocks. The new rocks have changed from sedimentary to metamorphic to igneous and are ready to repeat the cycle.

Below: Canary Spring, Mammoth Hot Springs, is named for the yellow color of its sulfur deposits of filamentous bacteria.   PHOTO BY JEFF FOOTT

a gas. Superheated water rises as steam and escapes at the surface through cracks in the earth. This type of activity is called a fumarole, or steam vent. When more water is added to the formula, the cooler water from above traps heated water below, the steam becomes more and more pressurized until the lower levels of

Right: Liberty Cap, at 37 feet tall, is the remains of a hot spring cone long dormant. It was named by the Hayden Survey in 1871.
PHOTO BY TERRY DONNELLY

steam virtually explode, forcing water above the steam to shoot upwards and out of the vent, creating a geyser.

The most powerful of Yellowstone geysers is called Steamboat Geyser and is located in the Norris Geyser Basin. Steamboat Geyser may not erupt very often but when it does it fires a volley of water 300 to 350 feet into the air.

Norris Geyser Basin, near Norris Junction, features hundreds of geysers, hot springs and pools in its two distinct areas: Back Basin and Porcelain Basin. Back Basin has the spectacular Steamboat Geyser, as well as the acidic Echinus Geyser. An unusual feature of Echinus is its acidic water which is almost as acidic as vinegar. The Porcelain Basin geysers include Constant Geyser, which erupts several times each hour and tosses streams of water from 10 to 40 feet upwards, and Africa, a constantly

THE HAYDEN SURVEY EXPEDITION...

On January 19, 1871, Nathaniel P. Langford gave a lecture on the many wonders of a place called Yellowstone. Langford had been a member of the Washburn exploration party and gave a series of lectures based upon his personal notes made while exploring the region.

Attending the January 19th lecture was then head of the U. S. Geological Survey of the Territories, Dr. Ferdinand V. Hayden. Hayden felt that the area described by Langford warranted official exploration and requested Congress fund a survey expedition to the region. His request was granted and the Sundry Civil Act of March 3, 1871 allowed $40,000 for the exploration of "The sources of the Missouri and Yellowstone Rivers."

The survey team included Hayden's right-hand man, James Stevenson; artist Henry W. Elliott; a topographer named Anton Shoenborn and his assistant, A.J. Smith; an entomologist named Professor Cyrus Thomas; photographer William H. Jackson and assistant, George B. Dixon; meteorologist J.W. Beaman; several general assistants, a zoologist, a couple of botanists and mineralogist, Dr. Albert C. Peale. The world famous artist, Thomas Moran, was a guest of the party, representing the Northern Pacific Railroad Company. The Hayden Survey also included approximately twenty men who acted as general laborers.

An additional exploration party, consisting of Captain John W. Barlow and Captain David P. Heap, from the Corps of Engineers, along with several assistants, had been sent by General Philip H. Sheridan to meet up with Hayden and his survey party at Fort Ellis.

The Hayden Survey left Fort Ellis on July 15, 1871, and the two groups met up at Mammoth Hot Springs. After a short rest they continued through the Washburn Range to the upper and lower waterfalls of the Yellowstone River. They crossed the Yellowstone River near Mud Volcano and camped on the shore of Yellowstone Lake

Hayden survey party in camp c1871.
PHOTO COURTESY OF NATIONAL PARK SERVICE, YELLOWSTONE NATIONAL PARK

on July 28. All along the way the topographers and engineers made note of the lay of the land while the botanists and geologists gathered specimens, and the photographers took pictures. Both Hayden and Barlow gave names to dozens of the natural features they came across, many of which are still in existence today.

Hayden's group followed along the shores of Yellowstone Lake to the southeast where they headed south, following Yellowstone River to Bridger Lake, which Hayden claimed didn't exist. He was wrong, there is in fact a Bridger Lake.

Captain Barlow's group followed the Heart River to the Snake River before heading east towards the Yellowstone River. Both parties then turned north, although each party took its own route, the Hayden party left Yellowstone on August 26, with Barlow following him two days later. August 30th saw the return of Hayden's party to Fort Ellis, the Barlow group reached the fort on September 1, ending what would become the most comprehensive survey of Yellowstone.

The results of the exploration and survey by the Barlow and Hayden parties are still felt today. They returned from Yellowstone with enough information to complete an accurate map, even though much of Barlow's information was lost in the Chicago fire of 1871. Luckily, Captain Heap had taken his topographic notes and his other observations to his office in St. Paul where he was able to create the first accurate map showing the correct placement of the area's features in relationship to both longitude and latitude.

The information compiled on Yellowstone by the Barlow and Hayden surveys became more important than ever when Hayden returned to his Washington D.C. office to find a letter from A.B. Nettleson asking Hayden to recommend in his official report that the Great Geyser Basin be forever reserved as a public park. And that is exactly what happened.

Above: A heart shaped hot spring in the Lower Geyser Basin. The substance surrounding this hot spring is geyserite, also known as siliceous sinter. The orange color away from the geyser's edge is the result of algae growing in strands in runoff water that has cooled down.
PHOTO BY JEFF FOOTT

erupting geyser. Dark Cavern Geyser, another Porcelain Basin geyser, erupts almost as often as Constant Geyser but shoots its stream of hot water only 11 to 20 feet high. Many of these geysers can be experienced on an easy two-mile walk along Porcelain Geyser Trail.

Because of the constant geothermal activity in the Norris Geyser Basin area it is common for changes to occur. Sometimes active geysers will become dormant while new hot springs appear, a result of changes in the underground plumbing structure. This unpredictability adds another facet to Yellowstone's puzzling story.

Old Faithful is the most popular of all of the geysers in Yellowstone, and in the rest of the world. One of the reasons Old Faithful is so popular is due to its consistency. It has been known for eruptions of about 130 feet in height and it has erupted an average of 22 times a day, each and every day, ever since the white man has paid attention. Each time it erupts, it shoots an average of 5000 to 8000 gallons of water high into the air, one of Yellowstone National Park's most popular tourist events.

The Old Faithful Area includes much more than Old Faithful itself. There are several other

Above: Runoff from Excelsior Geyser heats the Firehole River keeping it free from ice in winter.   PHOTO BY JEFF FOOTT

high. Lone Star Geyser erupts about every 3 hours with 20 to 30 foot plumes of water that last for about 25 minutes. An interesting feature of Lone Star is its twelve foot high cone.

Another very popular feature in the area near Old Faithful is Emerald Pool, a beautiful deep green pool that gets its colors from the yellow algae that grows in the pool. As the yellow algae and deep blue color of the sky reflected in the water are combined they create the stunning color that gives the pool its name. Rimming

Above: Stair-step deposits of travertine at Minerva Terrace in the Mammoth Hot Springs area formed as mineral laden waters overflowed the spring.
PHOTO BY DICK DIETRICH

Above: Fishing Cone, West Thumb Geyser Basin. Once a popular tourist attraction, it was said you could catch a trout in Lake Yellowstone and cook it in the boiling water of Fishing Cone without ever taking it off your hook. Because of injuries in the past, fishing here is no longer allowed.
PHOTO BY ART WOLFE

fairly consistent geysers in this area, one of which is Plume Geyser which goes off every 25 to 27 minutes, shooting water 25 to 30 feet

Right: Beauty Pool in Upper Geyser Basin. Pool colors are a result of water temperatures. Blue reflects the sky in water too hot to grow algae or bacteria. At 167°F yellow bacteria appear. As temperatures drop orange, green and brown will appear. Those in the know can tell how hot a hot springs is just by its color.
PHOTO BY MARY LIZ AUSTIN

the pool are stripes of orange and yellow that are also caused by algae. Hot pool colors are determined by the algae or bacteria growing in them. When the water is too hot nothing can survive. As the water cools a broad spectrum of

Above: Sand Point at the mouth of Flat Mountain Arm, Yellowstone Lake. Yellowstone Lake, the largest high-altitude natural freshwater lake in the United States, covers 136 square miles of the national park and has 110 miles of shoreline. In its deepest areas, near West Thumb, it is more than 320 feet deep.   PHOTO BY FRED HIRSCHMANN

colors appear beginning with yellow bacteria which appear at 167° F. As temperatures cool several more degrees orange, green and brown colors will appear.

Giantess Geyser, located in the Old Faithful area, is a dramatic geyser that shoots boiling water 100 to 200 feet into the air. When the Giantess Geyser erupts, the ground shakes from the force of the explosions from deep underground. Although Giantess does not erupt very often, when it does it often lasts from 12 to 35 hours.

One of the more interesting thermal experiences in the Old Faithful area is Riverside Geyser, located along the banks of Firehole River. When Riverside erupts, around every six or seven hours, it shoots a 75 ft. stream of water in an arch over the Firehole River.

These are just a few of the spectacular wonders of the thermal features of Yellowstone. There are so many it is hard to decide which to see first. Keep in mind, they are apt to change without notice as conditions in the area change.

Millions of years of volcanic activity created the thermal features which have made the park famous around the world, but they were not

the only forces working on the landscape we find today. Coinciding with the great caldera eruptions the Yellowstone region was involved with the same periods of glaciation that lay across the northern regions. Although the giant ice sheets from the north did not travel as far south as Yellowstone, the area formed its own glaciers during these same periods.

At its maximum, the Yellowstone ice fields covered much of the area now comprising the park. In the area that is now Yellowstone Lake the ice reached 4000 feet thick. As the ice fields thickened, they started to move, pushing rock material in front, they scoured deep cuts in the valleys, trimmed the mountains and left rock, gravel, silt and sand many miles from their original locations.

Above: Large boulders in the middle of Gibbon River on an early morning in September. Erosion by running water is the most significant of all erosive forces.   PHOTO BY JEFF GNASS

Volcanism, glaciation and all of the forces of erosion that shaped Yellowstone in the past are continuing to sculpt the region today. Another caldera eruption will more than likely take place in the future, perhaps within the next 100,000 years, and the of forces erosion will once again quietly reshape the new landscape.

Left: These large granite boulders now lying in the grassy Lamar Valley are examples of glacial erratics, rocks moved far from their original deposits as glaciers moving through the region pushed them along and finally left them behind as the glaciers melted away.
PHOTO BY CARR CLIFTON

Right: Waterfall designs at Rustic Falls on the Gardner River, Yellowstone National Park. Rustic Falls was named by Yellowstone National Park Superintendent Philetus W. Norris in 1879.
PHOTO BY JEFF GNASS

WILDLIFE

Perhaps the most comprehensive ecologically undisturbed area remaining in the continental United States, Yellowstone National Park is a model for animal protection rights and proudly proclaims itself "the largest wildlife sanctuary in the United States."

Enforcement of the park's wildlife protection policies was not always practiced. In the late 1800s great herds of elk, *Cervus canadensis,* and bighorn sheep, *Ovis canadensis,* were killed, and the once plentiful bison, *Bison bison,* came perilously close to being extirpated (completely wiped out) by greedy hunters and poachers. Alarmed at the damage to the area's animal populations, Congress passed the Lacy Act in 1894, making hunting in the park illegal.

Because the concept of preservation was just being formed, the early days of tourism in Yellowstone saw the exploitation of many of the park's animals. Bear cubs were tied up and displayed for the enjoyment of visitors, and regular bear feedings took place every day at the park dumps, making the bears dependent upon man for their food. Unfortunately, these encounters between bears and humans led to the destruction of many bears who became aggressive towards humans in their search for food, a bad situation for humans and bears.

Today, wildlife preservation is an important part of the Yellowstone experience. The park's elk populations have recovered to the point where more than 25,000 elk, or wapiti, can be found traveling through the park in summer time. The black bear, *Ursus americanus,* and grizzly bear, *Ursus horribilis,* populations are also recovering. Certain areas within the park, called bear management areas, heavily restrict hiking during certain times of the year so that contact between humans and bears, of both species, is kept to a minimum.

Mule deer, *Odocoileus hemionus,* moose, *Alces alces,* badger, *Taxidea taxus,* and bighorn sheep, *Ovis canadensis,* are found throughout Yellowstone. Less common are beavers, *Castor canadensis,* which were trapped to near extinction during the last century, as were cougars, *Felis concolor,* also known as mountain lions, elusive predators who do their best to avoid humans but can be quite dangerous if encountered. Cougars can sometimes be spotted along the banks of the Yellowstone River.

Yellowstone National Park supports many types of animal habitats, from the riparian (streamside) environments where you will find river otter, *Lutra canadensis,* and beaver, to the treelines of the alpine tundra where the bighorn sheep spend their summers grazing.

Other Yellowstone wildlife includes a variety of mammals including pronghorn, *Antilocapra americana,* moose, *Alces alces,* mink, *Mustela vison,* marten, *Martes americana,* Uinta chipmunk, *Eutamias umbrinus,* red fox, *Vulpes fulva,* bobcat, *Lynx rufus,* and yellow-bellied marmot, *Marmota flaviventris,* who spend their summers munching on wildflowers. All in all, Yellowstone National Park provides habitat

Yellowstone National Park is home to two bear species, black bear, *Ursus americanus,* and the larger grizzly bear, *Ursus horribilis.* Not all black bears have black coats, many have coats that are brown, cinnamon or blond. Mature black bears weigh between 200-600 pounds while the adult grizzlies weigh between 400-1500 pounds. All bears are capable of aggressive behavior and should be given a wide berth, especially when accompanied by their cubs. Both species go into partial hibernation from November to April.

Left: Rocky Mountain elk, *Cervus canadensis,* or wapiti, in fall rut. Mature bulls may weigh more than 1000 pounds and stand as high as five feet at the shoulder with a body length of up to ten feet long. Females are around twenty-five percent smaller than males at maturity.
PHOTO BY JEFF FOOTT

Right: Gray wolf, *Canis lupus,* running through snow. Wolves were reintroduced to Yellowstone in 1995. Travelling in packs of between two and twenty members, wolves may travel as far as forty miles in a day searching for prey.
PHOTO BY LEN RUE, JR.

for more than sixty-five species of mammals.

The most controversial mammal in the park is the gray wolf, *Canis lupus*. The largest member of the dog family, the gray wolf in no way resembles the mean, vicious animal portrayed in many fairy tales. While most wolves can kill with skillful precision, they can also be very social.

Traveling in packs from 2 to as many as 20 wolves, each wolf in the pack has its own distinct personality. It is not uncommon for the healthiest of pack wolves to offer their kill to another wolf who is too sick or old to hunt on its own.

Gray wolves can grow up to 6 feet long, from the tip of the tail to the end of the nose. Males can weigh as much as 100 lbs. and stand about 30 inches tall at the shoulder. The females are generally slightly smaller than the males.

Wolves come in several different colors ranging from white to dark black. Wolves in Yellowstone are a mixture of colors, with gray the predominant color. The underbelly and legs of the wolf are generally lighter in color. Their coat is made up of two layers, the soft under fur is protected by long guard hairs that prevent moisture from getting to the thick under fur. Climate dictates the thickness of the coat, most wolves shed a portion of both coats in the spring, only to have them grow back as winter approaches.

Wolves are built to run. Their slim hips, deep chest and strong legs allow them to run for

Above: Coyote, *Canis latrans*, standing in fresh snow. Coyote are fairly common year-round and can be found parkwide. PHOTO BY LEN RUE, JR.

Above: A badger, *Taxidea taxus*, peers around a lichen covered rock. Badgers have short legs with long claws used to burrow. Carnivorous, badgers are quite aggressive when cornered.
PHOTO BY JEFF FOOTT

REINTRODUCTION OF WOLVES TO YELLOWSTONE...

Wolf reintroduction is probably the most controversial subject in Yellowstone. Historically, there has never been a more persecuted animal than the wolf. Centuries of fairy tales have portrayed the wolf as a ruthless man-eater. In fact, no documented case of death caused by healthy wild wolves exists since the beginning of record keeping in North America. Hunted to near extinction, the wolf was placed on the endangered species list in 1973. Once tens of thousands of wolves roamed America but by the end of 1995 less than 2500 remained in the continental United States.

Although the wolf reintroduction process in Yellowstone began in the 1970s, it was not until 1995 that reintroduction actually took place. After years of legal action by ranchers and farmers of Idaho, Wyoming and Montana, who tried to prevent wolf reintroduction because they feared harm to their livestock, the Final Environmental Impact Statement regarding the reintroduction was issued in May 1994, making final the decision to restore the gray wolf to Yellowstone.

In January of 1995, 18 wolves captured in northwestern Canada were transported to the U.S. Four wolves were released in Idaho and fourteen were bound for specially built holding pens in Yellowstone. By January all the wolves had been transferred to three acclimatization pens. The pens, at Crystal Creek, Soda Butte and Rose Creek, allowed the wolves to adjust to their surroundings. The wolves, closely monitored, were fed road-killed deer and elk.

After two months of acclimatization they were released. The gate of the Crystal Creek pen was opened on March 21, 1995, but because the wolves associated the gate with humans they would not use it for an exit. Finally, a hole was cut in the rear of the fence and the wolves left to begin new lives. Wolves in the

Above: Gray wolf, *Canis lupus*, the largest member of the canine family, were reintroduced in the park in 1995, after decades of debate between ranchers and environmentalists. PHOTO BY JEFF FOOTT

other pens were released soon after, making a total of 14 released in the park in 1995. In 1996, 11 more were released in the Yellowstone area.

Since reintroduction there have been many wolf sightings. Wolf movement has been monitored with the help of radio collars placed on the wolves during relocation. Crystal Creek wolves were spotted in the Lamar and Pelican Valleys inside the park but have also traveled outside the park to the adjacent national forests, as did Soda Butte and Rose Creek wolves.

Despite the dire predictions of ranchers and farmers, the relocated wolves have caused few problems. One male wolf killed two sheep and a dog was thought to have been killed. A group called Defenders of Wildlife compensated the rancher for the dead sheep and the wolf that killed the sheep was captured and relocated back into the park. More widely reported was the killing of one of the wolves by a Montana rancher who was arrested and since convicted of violating the Endangered Species Act.

long hours every day. Many packs travel as much as 40 miles every day.

Wolves have an excellent sense of smell and their sharp hearing is remarkable. Some scientists believe that wolves hunt as much by sound as they do by smell. These skills help the wolf search for prey. Built for a feast-or-famine lifestyle, the wolf can go for several days without eating and then gorge on over a dozen pounds of meat at one time. Wolves spend a third of their lives hunting. They will make a meal of almost every part of the prey, including bones and marrow. The exception is the stomach of the prey, which must seem unappetizing to the wolves who leave them for scavengers. Wolves will also eat rodents, rabbits, fish, berries and insects. Consumption of grasses and large quantities of water are very important to the gray wolf's health.

Wolves live in complicated social structures. The dominant male is known as the alpha male and he controls the pack with the help of the dominant, or alpha female. The alpha

Above: Pronghorn, *Antilocapra americana,* in a field of grass in Yellowstone National Park. Often called pronghorn antelope, the pronghorn is not an antelope but is the last remaining member of the family Antilocapridae, a group of species that has been around for 20 million years. Pronghorn rely on their great speed, they are the swiftest animals in North America, to escape predators and are able to sprint at speeds near 75 miles per hour and sustain speeds of 40 miles per hour over great distances. Both the male and female of the species have horns.
PHOTO BY GLENN VAN NIMWEGEN

wolves often mate, although other males in the pack will sometimes mate with the alpha female. The alpha female chases away other females who may try to mate with dominant males of the pack. This controlled mating keeps

Above: A yellow-bellied marmot, *Marmota flaviventris,* stands on his hind legs and surveys his domain. Marmots hibcrnatc in September and reappear in March, when they bear their young. They feed on wildflowers and grasses.
PHOTO BY JEFF FOOTT

pack numbers reasonable.

The mating season usually takes place at winter's end. In the spring, a week or two before she is ready to whelp, the alpha female looks for a suitable den. If she cannot find a safe den she may dig a shelter herself.

After a gestation period of 63 days the alpha female produces a litter of up to as many as 13 pups, although 4–5 is more common. Many pups don't survive infancy, often falling prey to severe weather, pups are also eaten by bears. If a pup shows signs of being either sick or weak, an adult wolf may kill them.

When the pups are ready to leave the den, at about two months old, they are taken to one of several strategic sites, allowing the pack to hunt. The whole pack contributes to feeding and raising the pups. When the pups are older they are taken on hunts with the adults who teach them the hunting skills they will need in order to survive.

Once the pups are a year old they may be ready to leave the pack. A yearling may join another pack, travel alone, or stay with the

Below: Bison, *Bison bison,* gathering around a hot spring for warmth during mid-winter in the Lower Geyser Basin.
PHOTO BY JEFF FOOT

parental pack for another year. Wolf pups do not become sexually mature until they reach about two years of age.

Above: Bull moose, *Alces alces.* The largest member of the deer family, full grown males may weigh more than 900 lbs. and reach ten feet in length.   PHOTO BY GLENN VAN NIMWEGEN

Communication between wolves consists of three parts; *olfactory, postural signaling* and *vocalization*. The highly developed *olfactory skills* of the wolf enables them to use scent marking to identify territorial boundaries and identify other members of the pack when they are apart. Also, evaluating scent markings allows them to determine what has taken place within a specific area, a hunt for example. Wolves on the move leave their own scent marks, or check for other scent markings once every couple of minutes. It is also thought that scent marking allows lone wolves to find other loners for the purpose of mating or to create new packs.

Wolf *postural communication* consists of both body language and facial expression. Dominant wolves use aggressive body language, such as an erect stance with a direct stare and a raised tail, to indicate that he is dominant. A submissive wolf might respond by lowering its body, laying back its

Above: A North American beaver, *Castor canadensis,* towing a food branch. Beavers may burrow in river banks or build dams depending on their location. They live in close family groups including a male, a female and their young.   PHOTO BY LEONARD LEE RUE III

THE BEAR FACTS...

Yellowstone National Park is home to two species of bears; black bear, *Ursus americanus,* and grizzly bear, *Ursus horribilis.* Black bear are the most common and can be found almost anywhere in the park, as can the less common grizzly bear.

Black bears are not always black. A full half of all black bears in the park are shades of brown, cinnamon or sometimes blond. A mature black bear may weigh between 200 and 600 pounds. Both species can be very aggressive, especially females with their cubs. For those who have heard tales of climbing trees to escape mature bears, forget it. Even adults of both species can climb trees, not just cubs.

In the last century an estimated 100,000 grizzly bears roamed the land between the Pacific Coast and the Mississippi River. Today, only about 1000 grizzlies survive in the continental United States, with an estimated 200 to 300 living within the Yellowstone ecosystem. In 1975, the grizzly was given federal protection and placed on the Endangered Species list.

The size of the grizzly bear can vary widely, weighing 400-1500 pounds and average 6-9 feet long, and up to 9 feet tall when standing on their hind feet. Their fur ranges from dark brown to blond and, unlike black bear fur, is silver at the tips, giving them a grizzled appearance.

Bears are omnivorous and may eat 25–35 pounds of food a day. Their diet consists mostly of plants and berries. Favorite foods include whitebark pine nuts, roots, moths, ants and fish. Grizzly bears also hunt deer, bison and elk.

Grizzly bears can easily be identified from black

Above: Black bear, *Ursus americanus,* approaches a stream for a drink. Although bears resemble big, friendly dogs they are quite dangerous, with mature males weighing between 200 and 600 pounds.   PHOTO BY JEFF FOOTT

bears by the hump between their shoulders and their dish-shaped face. Both species generally stay to themselves, except for mothers and cubs and siblings. They will attack a human if they feel threatened, provoked, are forced to defend their cubs, or food, or if wounded. Their strong bodies, quick speed, and long claws and teeth make them a formidable foe. Their only enemies are other bears and man.

Cubs are born between January and March and remain with the mother for as long as 4 1/2 years, usually heading out on their own in the spring of their third year. Mothers protect their cubs by chasing them up a tree.

Right: A grizzly bear, *Ursus horribilis,* keeps a wary eye on photographer Len Rue. Grizzlies have killed many people.   PHOTO BY LEN RUE, JR.

Bears hibernate for about five months every winter, usually starting in October or November. They prepare for their long sleep by eating five times as much food as normal from late summer until they enter their dens. This is called hyperphagia and it allows the bears to build enough fat reserves to last them throughout the winter. Bears look for dens in remote areas situated to protect them from the fierce winter winds. While in hibernation they don't eat or drink. Their body fat is used as fuel for their body and, while their respiration and heart rates drop radically, body temperature only lowers a few degrees. Bears are not true hibernators, they are partial hibernators and will wake up if they are disturbed.

The greatest threat to the once plentiful grizzly bear is the destruction of habitat caused by over logging and construction of too many roads. Stronger efforts need to be implemented in order to protect this species and Yellowstone National Park is trying to help. Some backcountry areas of Yellowstone are off limits to hikers in order to prevent contact between bears and humans, thus ensuring a longer life for all concerned.

ears and dropping its tail, all indications of submissiveness. These actions, along with cheek rubbing, muzzle mouthing, rolling over on the back– and many other types of body language not yet understood by man– all seem to contribute to the well being and harmony of the wolf pack.

The third type of communication between wolves is *vocalization*. There are many reasons that wolves howl. They may be searching for their pack, or members of their pack, or sending an alarm or a message to other pack members. Howling often takes place during mating season. When one wolf howls, others in the pack will often join in. When wolves howl together they harmonize, this creates the impression of a great number of howling wolves when there are really only a few.

parts of the world but because they were considered a threat to man they were systematically destroyed. In the United States they came dangerously close to extinction in the mid 1900s. After extensive study by a number of dedicated individuals, mankind has become aware of the value of these animals in our ecosystems. The reintroduction of

Right: A cow elk, *Cervus canadensis,* cleans a newborn calf. Elk calves are usually born in early summer, weighing between 20 and 40 lbs. at birth.
PHOTO BY GLENN VAN NIMWEGEN

Above: Great gray owl's, *Strix nebulosa,* eyes are fixed in their head. In order to focus on a subject they must turn their head. Great gray owls have wingspans of up to five feet. They are one of two species of owl with yellow eyes and no ear tufts.
PHOTO BY JEFF FOOTT

Other vocalizations include barking, growling and whining, again, they may use this method of communication for any number of reasons. These sounds are also used for communication with pups, although growling can occur during angry confrontations between adults.

Wolves once roamed freely throughout most

Right: Mule deer, *odocoileus hemionus,* in velvet, standing in a field of wildflowers. Only bucks, which weigh between 100 and 475 pounds, have antlers. Mule deer browse on a variety of trees, shrubs and grasses and enjoy eating acorns.
PHOTO BY GLENN VAN NIMWEGEN

WILDLIFE CONTINUED...

wolves to Idaho and Yellowstone is only the beginning. Plans are being made to reintroduce wolves in many places around the world.

Birds are more prevalent in the park than mammals, due to migration. A few of the more notable birds are; the majestic great blue heron, the once almost extinct trumpeter swan, several types of grebes, pelicans, ibises, cormorants, loons, many different species of ducks, geese and hawks. Falcons, nuthatches, cranes, plovers, hummingbirds, coots, grouse, quail, pheasant, woodpeckers, doves, owls, dippers, flycatchers, sparrows, larks, terns, sandpipers, wrens, swallows, finches, warblers and the American symbol, the bald eagle all make their home, for at least part of the year, in Yellowstone National Park.

As might be expected in an area with such harsh winters, there are relatively few types of amphibians in Yellowstone. There are bullfrogs, northern leopard frogs, spotted frogs, and striped chorus frogs

and not to be forgotten the western toad. Frogs survive the extremely cold, harsh winters of the Northern Rockies by hibernating in the mud at

Above: Mountain lion, *felis concolor,* or cougar, are the largest North American cats. A mature cougar can make a running leap of up to 39 feet.   PHOTO BY GLENN VAN NIMWEGEN

the bottom of small ponds around the park.

Reptiles in the park are limited to only a few types of lizards and snakes. There are just two

different kinds of garter snakes; the western terrestrial and common garter snakes, who can be found in the lower elevations of the park. Other reptiles include the western rattlesnake, sagebrush lizard, bullsnake, and the rubber boa snake. It is difficult for reptiles to survive the extremely cold weather of the park, but these snakes and lizards have adapted well to the Yellowstone environment.

Many of the lakes and streams in Yellowstone were originally free of fish because of the barriers formed by waterfalls. Today the lakes and streams have a wide variety of fish for the enjoyment of the anglers who love the beautiful scenery of Yellowstone. The only fish that is native to the area is the cutthroat trout, but other fish including brown trout, whitefish, Mackinaw Lake trout, rainbow trout, grayling, and brook trout were introduced to the lakes and rivers many years ago. Today, both the Yellowstone and Madison Rivers are consid-

Above: A bull elk, *Cervus canadensis,* wades into the Yellowstone River for a drink. In summer the park's elk population reaches 25,000 to 30,000.
PHOTO BY TOM DANIELSEN

ered two of the best trout fishing rivers in the United States.

Proper wildlife management is an essential ingredient in the continuing preservation of Yellowstone National Park. Park policies will ensure a pristine environment for visitors to enjoy viewing the wide variety of wildlife and natural wonders of Yellowstone, the world's first national park.

Left: A pair of red fox, *Vulpes vulpes,* stare from their den beneath the roots of a tree.
PHOTO BY JEFF FOOTT

Right: A black bear, *Ursus americanus,* stands on his hind legs to rub his back against a tree, either marking his scent or scratching an itch.
PHOTO BY ART WOLFE

FLORA...

Because the topography of the Greater Yellowstone Ecosystem is so diverse, the park, and the region that surrounds it, supports well over 1600 different species of plants. The Yellowstone area has remained relatively untouched by humans and exhibits a fairly unspoiled representation of the native plant species which have grown in this area for hundreds, possibly thousands, of years.

In the study of ecology, a science dealing with all living things, seven life zones were established between the equator and the North Pole in a study of flora and fauna formulated during the late nineteenth century by Clinton Hart Merriam for the United States Department of Agriculture. Merriam's study was based on the premise that a change of 1000 feet in elevation will have the same effect on plant life as changes of 300 to 500 miles in latitude. He also determined temperature drops 3.5 to 5 degrees for each 1000 foot rise in elevation.

Elevations in the park range from 11,358 feet at Eagle Peak, to 5282 feet at Reese Creek, with most of Yellowstone National Park lying between 7000 and 8500 feet.

The Transition Zone, between 5500 and 8500 feet, is host to shrubs and grasses including wheatgrass, saltbrush, greasewood and Junegrass. Even prickly pear cactus thrive in the drier low lying areas of Yellowstone. Although grasses that grow so well in the spring may appear dead in the fall, their root systems are still alive and just waiting for a rain shower to perk them up again. It is believed that grasses are able to survive for many years, perhaps even hundreds of years.

In the meadows wildflowers, Yellowstone's colorful gifts to summer visitors, dominate. From May to September wildflowers appear in almost every corner of the park's meadows and marshes. Northern bedstraw can be found blooming from July to August in the northern ranges, while Yellowstone Lake areas provide glimpses of delicate glacier lily, found in May and June. Wild strawberry, yarrow, arnica, aster, shooting star, harebell, and lupine can be found throughout park during the summer months.

Riparian areas (literally pertaining to banks of a natural course of water) support the most colorful deciduous tree species in the park, the cottonwoods. Several species of willow trees and cattails, alder, sedges and mosses can also be found in these very moist areas.

Douglas fir are found in the Transition and Canadian Life Zones, growing mostly between 6500 and 8000 feet, and sometimes higher. Lodgepole pine, the park's most common tree, grow in elevations from 7500 to 9000 feet.

Spruce and fir grow in the Hudsonian Life Zone, between 9500–12,000 foot elevations on south slopes, although they also grow in lower elevations. Alpine tunda is found in the highest elevations of the Greater Yellowstone Area with stunted growth showing evidence of the difficulty of survival in the harsh climate of the region's higher elevations.

The most prolific tree in Yellowstone National Park is the lodgepole pine, *Pinus contorta*, which covers more than 60 percent of Yellowstone. Although 80 percent of Yellowstone is forested, lodgepole pine is the most common conifer. One type has serotinous cones which will not release its seeds unless exposed to extreme heat, perfect for reforestation after forest fires.

Left: Lodgepole pine crowd the rocky banks of the scenic Kepler Cascades on the Firehole River in Yellowstone National Park.
PHOTO BY CARR CLIFTON

Right: Colorful spray of summer wildflowers in the rolling meadows of Yellowstone Valley. While valleys filled with verdant grasses, flowers and shrubs create a delightful picture, they also serve a greater purpose. Elk, bighorn sheep and bison all depend upon these shrubs and grasses for food. Many small animals use the meadow plants as feeding grounds or habitats, and they in turn are part of the food chain for coyotes, fox, snakes, raptors and other predators.
PHOTO BY TERRY DONNELLY

Flora Continued...

Above: August finds showy daisy, *Erigeron speciosus,* in bloom. Showy daisy grow to between one and three feet. They have 1.5–2 inch diameter flower heads with petals ranging from pink to white and yellow disks in their centers.
PHOTO BY RANDY A. PRENTICE

Above: Lichen adorns a rock in a meadow full of wildflowers near the Blacktail Plateau. Lichen are components of fungus and algae and are able to grow from rock surfaces without soil. The algal component manufactures the lichen's food by photosynthesis while the fungal component clings to the rock's surface and absorbs minerals. Lichen are known to live for decades.
PHOTO BY TERRY DONNELLY

Left: A field of lupine on The Promontory Point at Yellowstone Lake with Mt. Stevenson in the distance. Yellowstone Lake, the largest mountain lake in the continental United States, completely freezes over in winter. The cold waters of the lake decrease average temperatures in its vicinity by as much as five degrees.
PHOTO BY WILLARD CLAY

Above: Yellow flowers and shiny green leaves of Rocky Mountain pond lily, *Nuphar luteum,* interspersed among reflections of lodgepole pines, *Pinus concorta,* burned in the summer fires of 1988. The blaze of pink seen at the top is fireweed, *Epilobium angustifolium,* emerging under the pines.
PHOTO BY TOM DANIELSEN

Above: Calypso orchid, *Calypso bulbosa,* in full bloom. These delicate orchids are also known as fairy slippers, perfectly illustrated by this photo.
PHOTO BY JEFF FOOTT

Right: Larkspur, *Delphinium nuttallianum,* and composites at Swan Lake Flat, find themselves under a blanket of snow in June. Snow may fall in any month in Yellowstone National Park.
PHOTO BY GLENN VAN NIMWEGEN

THE FESTIVAL OF FALL...

Fall comes early to Yellowstone National Park– different elevations experience the changing of the seasons at different times– with the highest elevations finding deciduous trees turning colors as early as August. From delicate spring colors to the full-leaved, bright greens of summer the leaf builds in intensity for its show of fall color. Of all seasons, fall features the most spectacular and dramatic displays of color in the life cycle of a plant.

Fall represents the culmination of the life cycle of a leaf. Before a leaf falls from the tree, all its valuable remaining minerals and nutrients are transported from the leaf into the tree to avoid their loss. As soon as this process begins, the leaf stops producing chlorophyll, the substance that is responsible for its green color, to conserve energy and existing nutrients left in the leaf.

As the chlorophyll gradually fades away, the other pigments that were present in the leaf begin to show through. The yellow colors we see are the product of xanthophyll, while the red and orange colors are created by the presence of carotene, minerals that gain vibrancy as the chlorophyll fades.

Fall color is further enhanced by chemical reactions in the leaf producing anthocyanins, resulting in blue, scarlet or purple pigments, manufactured from the sugars that remain in the leaf after the nutrient supply has been denied. As the colors of anthocyanins are added to the xanthophyll and carotenes, they blend to create the full spectrum of fall colors.

The process of renewal in the plant's life cycle begins anew as its discarded leaves fall to the ground surrounding its own roots. The cast off and decomposing leaves contain large amounts of mineral salts–

Above: Fall colors on a red-tinted geranium, *Geranium maculatum,* form a background for delicate bluebells, *Campanula uniflora.*
PHOTO BY RANDY PRENTICE

including sulfur, iron, calcium, phosphorous, potassium, magnesium and other elements essential to the rebirth of the plant during

Above: A light dusting of snow covers the fall leaves of mountain ash, *Sorbus scopulina,* in Teton Pass.   PHOTO BY JEFF FOOTT

the following spring. As the leaves decay on the ground above the plant's roots, their minerals seep into the soil and are absorbed by the root system. Nature's own fertilizer.

Leaves begin changing colors in the early fall as photoperiodism– a phenomenon timing the major events in the lives of plants such as their flowering, opening of leaf buds and the appearance of fruit– sends a signal to the plant to start the chemical changes that in turn begin to alter the leaf's color.

Photosynthesis, the chemical process that gives plants the ability to produce glucose for use as their own food using a combination of water, light, carbon dioxide and heat is stopped until spring brings forth a new crop of leaves, to once again begin manufacturing chlorophyll and complete the cycle.

Left: Quaking aspen, *Populus tremuloides,* on the Blacktail Plateau, Yellowstone National Park.
PHOTO BY WILLARD CLAY

Right: Morning light illuminates aspen trees near Tower Falls. After leaves fall they decompose in soil below the tree and their minerals seep back into the soil to be absorbed by the tree's roots.
PHOTO BY WILLARD CLAY

While it is said that winter can show its frosty face at almost any time of year, real winter conditions generally arrive in late October and early November, as the first measurable amounts of snow cover Yellowstone National Park's landscape.

Yellowstone is a spectacular winter wonderland. Waterfalls frozen in mid-air and trees, nearly unrecognizable when covered by frozen steam from a geyser, show how winter wraps its frozen arms around the landscape to create an other worldly place.

The geothermal features of the park never rest, no matter what the temperature. Geysers still erupt but with a bit more fanfare, due to the large amounts of steam colder temperatures create. Hot springs, fumaroles and mud pots still continue to act as they always do, steaming, bubbling and boiling. The contrast of colors, snow against an algae rimmed hot pool, offers an unforgettable scene.

Although winter in Yellowstone can be quite severe, with daytime temperatures hovering around freezing and nighttime temperatures often below zero, many visitors prefer to visit the park in winter. There are fewer visitors and a better opportunity to see some of the park's larger mammals. Elk and bison can be found in large numbers throughout the park in winter. The bison seem to enjoy the warmer areas near the geysers and hot springs, particularly along the Firehole River, and choose these areas for their wintering ground.

Most of the park's bird population migrates to warmer climates during the winter and both grizzly and black bears go into partial hibernation. Mountain lion, rodents, coyote, moose, owls and wolves as well as pronghorn, mule deer and bighorn sheep are all active during the winter. Visitors may be able to catch sight of one of these animals if they are patient.

Even though most of the park is closed to wheeled vehicles from early November to the first of May, snowmobile season runs from late December to early March. Snowmobiles can be rented at many locations both inside and out of the park and a seat on one of the many snowcoaches, busses with caterpillar tread or skis to move them over snow, can be a ticket into the park, reservations are suggested.

Most of Yellowstone lies between 7000 and 8500 feet and receives around 150 inches of snowfall per year. Higher elevations average about 50 inches more and can even reach 400 inches of snowfall in a season.

Since Yellowstone National Park consists of many types of terrains, from high mountain peaks reaching heights of more than 11,000 feet to the warmer lower valleys in the northern end of the park, weather conditions can vary depending upon the area. Most areas experience below freezing temperatures for most of the winter, although there are those occasions when the park experiences rather mild winter weather with temperatures reaching daytime highs in the 40s.

Left: Cattails and snow covered pines under a clearing winter sky at Nez Perce Creek. Winter brings an average of 150 inches of snow each year to Yellowstone National Park.
PHOTO BY TERRY DONNELLY

Right: Steam escapes a thermal vent encircled by snow in Yellowstone's Norris Geyser Basin. The clear winter day shows the snow covered Gallatin Mountain Range in the distance.
PHOTO BY MARY LIZ AUSTIN

Left: Winter dawn slowly brushes pastel colors over Castle Geyser's billowing steam.
PHOTO BY TERRY DONNELLY

Right: Frost covered trees of the Upper Geyser Basin where as much as 100 inches of snow can fall every year.
PHOTO BY TERRY DONNELLY

Below: Winter clouds begin to recede after dusting the valley with another layer of snow on the green waters of the Yellowstone River.
PHOTO BY TERRY DONNELLY

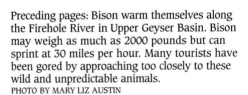

In 1988 wildfires raged throughout Yellowstone National Park burning almost 800,000 acres of the park's forests. Although evidence of these fires will be visible for many years to come, new growth has already begun to shows signs of the forests of the future.

In 1988 the complexion of Yellowstone was marred by fires that ravaged 793,800 acres in the national park, along with portions of the national forest lands bordering the park. Today, nearly a decade after the fires, we can see the evidence of reemerging life within the forest amid the destruction of the fires of 1988.

The conditions that led up to the fires of 1988 began piling up decades ago. When the National Park Service was first created one of its main functions was the prevention and suppression of forest fires. This intervention inhibited normal patterns of nature and more importantly, allowed the build-up of a thick carpet of combustible fuel that needed only a combination of extremely dry weather, high winds and a spark to set it ablaze.

In the early 1970s, Yellowstone changed its previous policy of putting out all fires and replaced it with a policy that allowed, under certain conditions, naturally occurring fires to burn out on their own. This policy was successful for over twenty years. Between 1972 and 1987 only 34,000 acres were burned by 235 naturally started fires, with the largest of the fires burning 7,400 acres.

Allowing the naturally started fires to burn removes years of accumulated biomass from the forest floor. The fire acts as a cleaning agent that sweeps through different levels of the forest burning everything it touches. Some trees survive, like pine trees which are protected by thick bark. Other trees cannot propagate without fire. The lodgepole pine have serotinous cones which will not release their seeds unless exposed to extreme heat.

Forest fires are particularly helpful for removing the undergrowth that competes with existing tall trees for water and soil nutrients. Fires return important minerals to the soil, providing the surviving trees with necessary nutrients for renewed growth.

In the summer of 1988 several fires, sparked by lightning, were burning in different areas of the park. Although the National Weather Service predicted less than normal rainfall and hotter than average temperatures, Yellowstone officials continued to allow naturally started fires that did not threaten human lives, visitor use areas or lands under the control of other agencies to burn freely, although they were closely monitored.

Trouble began outside the national park when lighting started a fire in the Storm Creek area of Montana's Custer National Forest on June 14, 1988. On June 23, trouble began in the park when a lightning strike started the Shoshone fire in the southwest corner of the park. More and more fires began to break out. There was the Fan fire, sparked on June 25 in the northwest corner of Yellowstone, and the Red fire which began on June 30, only a few miles from the Shoshone fire.

Several other natural fires were allowed to burn and did in fact go out on their own, but many fires just kept on burning and with the

Preceding pages: Bison warm themselves along the Firehole River in Upper Geyser Basin. Bison may weigh as much as 2000 pounds but can sprint at 30 miles per hour. Many tourists have been gored by approaching too closely to these wild and unpredictable animals.
PHOTO BY MARY LIZ AUSTIN

Left: Fireweed, *Epilobium angustifolium,* emerges under weathered trees in a burn area. Fireweed is among the first herbaceous species reestablished after forest fires.
PHOTO BY TERRY DONNELLY

Right: Clepsydra Geyser erupts at sunset against a backdrop of smoke and fire from forest fires during the first week of August 1988.
PHOTO BY GLENN VAN NIMWEGEN

SUMMER OF FIRE CONTINUED...

lack of rain and the increased winds most of these fires, including one carelessly started by a man with a chainsaw, continued their holocaust throughout the long, dry summer.

Finally, after a summer of smoke and ash, the fires cooled with the first snow of the season which fell on September 11. Although the fires continued to smolder well into November, winter weather finally put an end to the destructive fires of 1988.

Many of the area's buildings, homes and towns were threatened by the fires. Grant Village, Flagg Ranch, the Church Universal and Triumphant, the communities of Cooke City and Silver Gate, Canyon Village, West Yellowstone, Old Faithful Inn, Mammoth Hot Springs, Tower Villages and Lake Village were all threatened by the conflagration. Damage included a few ranches outside of Yellowstone, and more than

Above: The yellow flowers of Heartleaf arnica, *Arnica cordifolia,* carpet the forest floor amid charred remains of trees destroyed by the 1988 forest fires.
PHOTO BY JACK DYKINGA

twenty buildings within the park. Incredibly, there was no loss of human life in the battle against the fires that ultimately destroyed over 1.2 million acres in and around Yellowstone National Park. Animal casualties include hundreds of bison and elk and untold numbers of smaller animals. More than 9000 firefighters worked to overcome the forest fires that threatened the world's first national park with a cost to taxpayers of over $120 million.

Today, the cycle of forest life continues. New growth of fireweed, aster, grass and forb carpets the forest floor. Lodgepole pine and aspen are again growing throughout the forest. Wildlife has survived, and in some cases thrived as new growth on the forest floor allows better feeding for many species. Yellowstone tourism is even greater than it was before the fires of 1988, proving that life goes on.

Right: These burned trees below Mt. Washburn were victims of the conflagration of 1988.
PHOTO BY WILLARD CLAY

HUMAN HISTORY...

I t is commonly thought that small bands of hunters followed large grazing animals including mammoths, camels, horses, and giant sloths into the Yellowstone region more than 11,000 years ago via an ancient land bridge across the Bering Strait. At that time, nearly one-sixth of the world's surface was covered with ice. The formation of massive glaciers caused the oceans to recede and in some places sea level was lowered as much as 300 feet, exposing a 56 mile strip of the ocean's floor between northeastern Siberia and northwestern Alaska. This exposed land bridge, which allowed migratory access to the New World, occurred during the Pleistocene Epoch, or Ice Age.

In 1959, an obsidian projectile point was discovered near Yellowstone National Park. Its discovery suggests a presence of early hunters in and around Yellowstone sometime around 11,000 years ago. Evidence suggests that these early hunters lived in the higher elevations of the area. During this period it is probable that the area looked much as it does today, although lake levels may have been much higher due to runoff from departing glaciers.

As glaciers receded and the climate changed the early hunters were replaced by foragers. These foragers, whose diet consisted of berries, bugs, roots, lizards, snakes, fish and any small birds or animals they could catch, dominated most of the Yellowstone Plateau region from approximately 4000 B.C. until the first century A.D. It is likely that members of this early culture migrated from protected valleys, where they wintered, to the higher elevations of the mountains, where they spent their summers hunting and foraging. They hunted small and large game with spears and atlatls— a rigid board around two feet long with notches near the top in which the shafts of spears, darts or arrows, were inserted. The length of the atlatl extended the arm and increased the force behind the throwing of the projectile. Evidence of these peoples, in the form of several prehistoric hearths or fireplaces, has been found in Yellowstone Valley.

About the time of Christ the foraging people of the Yellowstone Plateau were replaced by another group of hunters. These late hunters adapted many of the hunting styles of their predecessors and began using the bow and arrow as well as building hunting blinds. The use of cooking vessels and grinding stones shows evidence of their sophistication.

The winter campsites discovered along the Yellowstone River, and summer camps scattered throughout the Yellowstone Plateau, has lead scientists to believe that the late hunters were not nomads, unlike their ancestors. The late hunters were able to hunt in small territories, enabling them to spend less time traveling and more time hunting. Seemingly an indication of a more comfortable lifestyle for the late hunters than that experienced by the more nomadic early hunters.

Right: Wildflowers surround a wooden bridge along the Lost Lake Trail.
PHOTO BY KATHY CLAY

Left: Fishing the Gibbon River in Yellowstone National Park. The only fish that is native to the area are cutthroat trout, but other fish including brown trout, whitefish, Mackinaw Lake trout, rainbow trout, grayling and brook trout were introduced to the region many years ago.
PHOTO BY DICK DIETRICH

By the end of the 17th century Yellowstone was surrounded by Kiowa, Flathead, Crow, and Shoshone Indian Tribes. Sometime in the 1700s the Shoshone obtained horses, probably from the Comanches who may have acquired them around the time of the southwestern Pueblo revolt in 1680. Horses were first brought to North America by Spanish Franciscan and Jesuit missionaries who tried to convert the Indians to Catholicism. Around this time, the Comanches often raided other tribes, as well as the Spanish settlements, and made away with many Spanish horses during these raids.

By the 1800s there were Piegans, part of the Blackfoot, in the areas from Musselshell River to the Continental Divide and north of the Yellowstone River. Crow Indians inhabited an area south of the Yellowstone River between

FLIGHT OF THE NEZ PERCE...

It could be said that the beginning of this tragic saga began with the arrival of the first white man to the Nez Perce homeland. The Nez Perce, named by French trappers who noted the Indians' penchant for pierced noses, lived peacefully near today's borders of Oregon, Idaho and Washington.

Their first experience with whites was the appearance of Lewis and Clark who traveled through the area in 1805. The tribe assisted the expedition by drawing maps and guiding the party as far as the Colombia River. They also cared for the expedition's horses until their return several months later.

Nez Perce Chief Joseph, in 1904.
COURTESY MONTANA HISTORICAL SOCIETY

Because of their positive experience with Lewis and Clark, and a few friendly white trappers, the Nez Perce trusted whites, and many became Christians. Unfortunately, the semi-nomadic life of the Nez Perce was not compatible with the white man's habit of dividing land into parcels for private ownership. Nez Perce believed no one owned the land, that the land offered its bounty to those reverent enough to reap the rewards offered by the earth, which they respected as a provider. They did not believe a person could sell something they did not own.

In the mid 1800s the rush of settlers following the Oregon Trail west were spreading out in all directions. It was inevitable that the settlers would eventually encroach upon Nez Perce lands.

The Nez Perce head chief in Wallowa Valley was Chief Joseph. Chief Joseph's own father, Old Joseph, had signed the treaty of 1855 which had pushed many smaller tribes off their lands and onto reservations, but guaranteed the Nez Perce more than seven million acres. This treaty was to last forever, or so Isaac Stevens, governor of the Washington Territory and superintendent of Indian affairs, assured the Indians.

Treaty or no treaty, white settlers continued to move onto Nez Perce lands, a frequent cause of friction. Only eight years after the treaty was signed, the government called a council to discuss reducing Nez Perce lands.

The Nez Perce had seen first hand the effects of fighting the whites. They had seen the decline of Cayuse and Wallawalla Indians from their homelands on the Columbia Plateau. They had seen Modocs stripped of their lands and shipped to reservations. Although the Nez Perce did not want to leave their homeland, they knew the futility of fighting the white man. Their world was turning white right before their eyes.

In 1863 a new treaty was signed, not by Old Chief Joseph or his son, but by others who said they represented all Nez Perce, consigning the Nez Perce onto a reservation a tenth as large as that of the 1855 treaty. Many tribes did go to the reservation, but many did not. Those who did not were considered non-treaty Indians and continued to live on their lands, ignoring the treaty. They believed that since they had not signed it, they weren't obligated to live up to the agreement. After many years of ignoring the treaty, ranchers and settlers were tired of sharing "their" land with the Nez Perce and urged the government to enforce the 1863 treaty and force the Nez Perce onto Idaho reservations.

Chief Joseph realized fighting the white man was only a temporary solution, as there seemed no end to their supply of soldiers, and reluctantly agreed to move his people to the reservation.

Unfortunately, a few hot headed warriors went on a drunken rampage and killed several whites, forcing the tribes of Chiefs Joseph and White Bird to avoid retaliation by fleeing. Before the tribes got very far they encountered their first military challenge. General O. O. Howard sent Captain David Perry, with some 125 enlisted men and volunteers, to fight the desperate Nez Perce. On the morning of June 17, 1877, exhausted soldiers met the Nez Perce in battle after traveling for two days. The Nez Perce were fresh and buoyed by chance of victory, after so many compromises with the white man. Perry and his troupe were exhausted, as were their horses. The Nez Perce easily fought off the soldiers and claimed victory over the white man and his army. Of course, their success was only temporary.

Chiefs Joseph and White Bird hoped to force Howard into a draw, and then reach a peaceful compromise. Instead, Howard and other whites in the northwest were concerned the Nez Perce would incite other displaced Indians and unite to form an undefeatable force. History shows this did not happen. Instead the Nez Perce continued to fight and flee, retreating from Howard's armies along Lolo Trail through the Bitterroot Mountains.

Once in Montana the Nez Perce believed they were out of trouble, leaving war with the whites behind in Idaho. Instead they were hunted and attacked by Colonel John Gibbon, and his force of about 165 men on August 9th.

Both sides suffered many casualties, although exact numbers are unknown, it is thought about 100 Nez Perce men, women and children were killed with dozens wounded. Casualties for the army came close to 30 dead and 40 wounded.

Instead of heading north for Canada, the Nez Perce still hoped to gain freedom by reaching the buffalo country east of Yellowstone. They headed south, raiding farms and ranches on the way and killing several people near Bannock Pass, before turning east towards the newly created park.

August 22, the Nez Perce entered Yellowstone National Park after traveling more than 1000 miles. Although exhausted from the effort, a few warriors found the energy to terrorize several parties of Yellowstone tourists. Two men were killed and two wounded by Nez Perce warriors who looted and burned any buildings they came across. Some captives escaped, and a few were released when the Chiefs discovered the young warriors' rash actions.

The Nez Perce spent almost two weeks in the park eluding both Colonel Samuel D. Sturgis and General Howard. Howard believed the Nez Perce could not escape the park because there were few ways out. He was determined to block them all.

Colonel Sturgis, who had been camped near Clarks Fork, believed the Indians were moving down the Shoshone and went south to head them off. This allowed Chief Joseph and his people to follow Dead Indian Gulch to Clarks Fork Canyon, very close to Sturgis's old camp. From there they left the park, and crossed the Yellowstone River, where they again fought off an army attack. They pressed northward toward Canada and what they hoped was freedom.

The Nez Perce believed they had so successfully fought off their enemy that they had time to stop and rest for a few days. This mistake cost them the war. They were less than 50 miles from the Canadian boarder when Colonel Nelson A. Miles and several companies of calvary launched an attack. Chief Joseph and his people fought back, although it is believed that hundreds of Nez Perce fled north during the fighting, safely reaching Canada.

During the standoff, Colonel Miles requested a meeting with Chief Joseph. Chief Joseph was captured by the Colonel's men who held him until they realized that one of their own men had been captured by the Nez Perce. The next day an exchange took place.

October 5, after more than 100 days and 1800 miles, Chief Joseph spoke the elegant words that remain his legacy, "From where the sun now stands I will fight no more forever."

COURTESY YELLOWSTONE NATIONAL PARK

the Absaroka-Wind rivers to the Powder River, and Shoshone occupied the areas west of the Absaroka Mountains and Wind River west to Oregon and south to Utah and Nevada.

The Nez Perce and Flathead Indians lived farther to the west. Nez Perce lived on the other side of the Bitterroot Mtns. in western Idaho as well as in parts of Washington and Oregon. Shoshone were so spread out that each subgroup lived very different from the others.

Shoshone, also called Sheepeaters, sitting inside a tepee in 1871.
COURTESY YELLOWSTONE NATIONAL PARK

From lush mountains and valleys of Wyoming and Montana to the high deserts of Utah and Nevada, the Shoshone subgroups were differentiated by diet. There were "buffalo eaters," "salmon eaters," "sheep eaters," and "root diggers." The buffalo hunters were at the top of the Shoshone social structure and the root diggers were at the bottom. Included in lower Shoshone social rungs were the Sheepeaters who hunted bighorn sheep. Sheepeaters were the only Native Americans to actually live in Yellowstone but several surrounding tribes, the Crows, Piegans and others often traveled and hunted in the area.

Philetus W. Norris
COURTESY YELLOWSTONE NATIONAL PARK

Typical of government at the time, Sheepeaters were never recognized as having a legitimate claim on the area and were eventually forced off their land about the time other Shoshone subgroups were forced onto the reservations. Yellowstone Sheepeaters joined the Shoshone chief, Washakie, and his tribe on Wind River Reservation in 1871.

The first white man to explore Yellowstone area was John Colter, a member of the famed Lewis and Clark Expedition of 1804-1806. In the winter of 1807-1808, Colter traveled about 500 miles on foot through the Yellowstone area as an employee of the Missouri Fur Trading Company, his mission was to tell local tribes of a new trading post at Fort Raymond on the Big Horn River.

An 1809 William Clark map shows Colter's route through the area. A marking of a place Colter called Hot Spring Brimstone, placed next to his crossing of the Yellowstone River, offers proof of his exploration.

The Northern Rockies teemed with wildlife in the 1820s, when the East could no longer provide the pelts necessary for the newly popular beaver hat, the fur traders sent trappers west, where the wildlife was still abundant.

David W. Wear
COURTESY YELLOWSTONE NATIONAL PARK

Mountain men spread out over the area and commenced a combined exploration and pillage of the area. After the area was pretty well trapped out the mountain men moved on, some to farming, while others acted as guides for exploration parties or the westward bound wagon trains. They were rough and ready with the skills needed to survive the harshest circumstances.

One of the lasting effects of the mountain men was the interest their stories created in Yellowstone. Imagine sitting around campfires listening to stories about bubbling mud pots or steaming vents that launched boiling water high into the sky. Stories told by

Two members of the Hayden Expedition survey party.
COURTESY YELLOWSTONE NATIONAL PARK

Below: Modern day explorer at Fairy Falls.
PHOTO BY JEFF FOOTT

Nathaniel Langford
COURTESY YELLOWSTONE NATIONAL PARK

mountain men were often chalked up to exaggeration, but on at least one occasion a listener decided to verify these accounts by going in search of the truth.

Warren Angus Ferris felt compelled to see for himself the wonders described by the trappers at a fur traders rendezvous. Ferris and a couple of Indian guides traveled to Yellowstone. Ferris, at one time a surveyor, was an educated man who kept a detailed account of his adventure, making his the first factual chronicle of Yellowstone. He was also the first to use the word "geyser" when describing Yellowstone's fountains.

Folsom, Cook and Peterson party began their exploration of Yellowstone in 1869. David E. Folsom, Charles W. Cook and William Peterson were miners. They entered the park on September 13, 1869.

They returned home on October 11th where they shared stories of great waterfalls, colorful canyons, picturesque valleys, deep bubbling pools and boiling water that shot straight into the air. Some of their stories were published, although the *New York Tribune* would not print the stories because "they had a reputation they could not risk with unreliable material."

August 22, 1870, General Henry Washburn, set out with the primary intention of obtaining publicity on the Yellowstone area. Financier Jay Cooke had plans to finance the Northern

Pacific Railroad and needed publicity to help raise funds for the financing. Included in the exploration party was Nathaniel P. Langford

Above: Cozy Heart Lake patrol cabin on a cold winter evening in Yellowstone National Park. PHOTO BY FRED HIRSCHMANN

who would later become Yellowstone's first park superintendent. Langford had agreed to gather material for a series of lectures on Yellowstone to serve as the publicity required by Jay Cooke & Company.

The greatest achievement of the Washburn party was a lecture given on January 19, 1871, by party member Nathaniel P. Langford that was heard by Dr. Ferdinand V. Hayden, then head of the U.S. Geological Survey.

Hayden, inspired by what he heard about the Yellowstone area, felt the area described by Langford should be officially explored and he asked Congress to fund an expedition. The Sundry Civil Act of March 3, 1871 allowed $40,000 for the exploration of "The sources of the Yellowstone and the Missouri rivers."

Hayden's survey included artist Henry W. Elliott; topographer Anton Shoenborn; entomologist Cyrus Thomas; photographer William H. Jackson and meteorologist J.W. Beaman. There were several general assistants, a zoologist, a couple of botanists and a mineralogist, Dr. Albert C. Peale. Famous artist Thomas Moran was a guest of the party and represented the Northern Pacific Railroad Company.

Another party, consisting of Captains John W. Barlow and David P. Heap, from the

Corps of Engineers had been sent by General Philip H. Sheridan to join Hayden's survey.

The Hayden Survey left Fort Ellis on July 15 and the Barlow party left on the 16th. Along the way topographers and engineers noted the lay of the land while botanists and geologists gathered specimens, and photographers took pictures. Hayden and Barlow named dozens of the natural features they came across, many still in existence today.

The information compiled by the two survey parties aided A. B. Nettleson in his efforts to have Great Geyser Basin forever reserved as a public park. On March 1, 1872, Congress designated Yellowstone "dedicated and set apart as a public park or pleasuring ground for the benefit and enjoyment of the people." By these words, Yellowstone became the world's first national park, a model for those to follow.

Nathaniel P. Langford, the first superintendent of Yellowstone, was an indifferent supervisor who did little to stop killing of wildlife within the park. He was replaced by Philetus W. Norris, a very dedicated superintendent, in 1877. When Norris endorsed a mail route from Mammoth

Above: Sunrise on Yellowstone Lake.
PHOTO BY FRED HIRSCHMANN

Hot Springs to Virginia City, Bozeman newspapers began a smear campaign that led to Norris' dismissal in 1882. Norris was followed by a succession of superintendents including, David W. Wear, that struggled to live up to Norris' standards. Finally, the U.S. Army was placed in control of Yellowstone until creation of the National Park Service in 1916.

Left: Old Faithful Inn silently watches over an eruption of Old Faithful Geyser in winter.
PHOTO BY FRED HIRSCHMANN

Right: Tower Creek rushes down a boulder laden streambed in Yellowstone National Park.
PHOTO BY CARR CLIFTON

Outside back cover: Steam venting from Castle Geyser under a winter sky.
PHOTO BY MARY LIZ AUSTIN